Cute IDEAS

WRITTEN BY
ROSIE PEET

MODELS BY
EMILY CORL AND ROD GILLIES

Contents

LET'S GET BUILDING!

Cool cactus

This cactus likes to take it easy. With its rounded base, it can rock on over to the desert to visit its cactus friends or rock itself to sleep for an afternoon siesta.

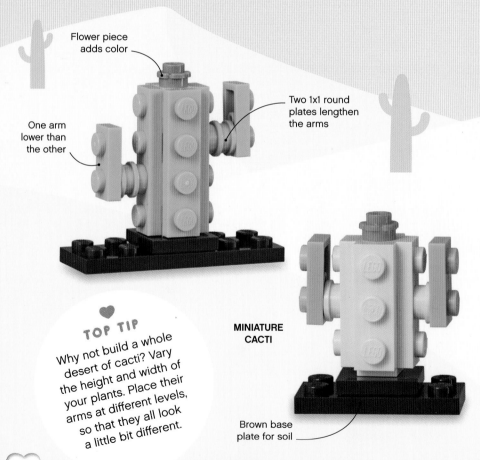

Flower piece adds color

Two 1x1 round plates lengthen the arms

One arm lower than the other

MINIATURE CACTI

Brown base plate for soil

TOP TIP

Why not build a whole desert of cacti? Vary the height and width of your plants. Place their arms at different levels, so that they all look a little bit different.

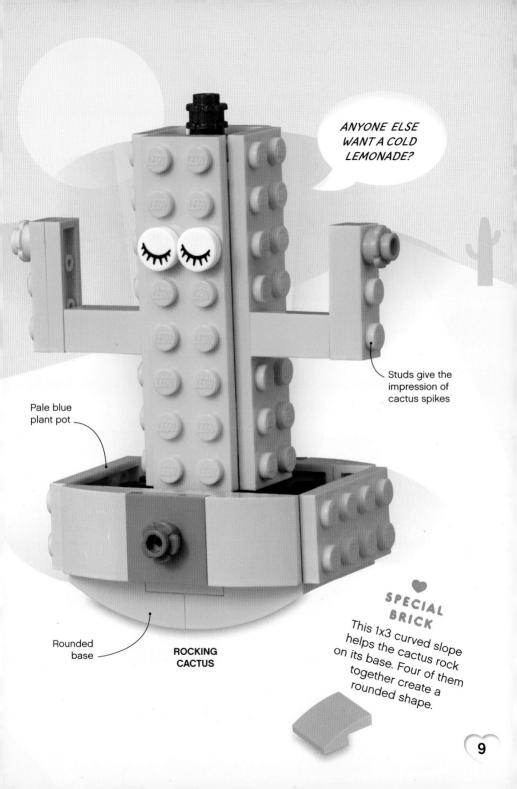

ANYONE ELSE WANT A COLD LEMONADE?

Studs give the impression of cactus spikes

Pale blue plant pot

Rounded base

ROCKING CACTUS

♥ SPECIAL BRICK

This 1x3 curved slope helps the cactus rock on its base. Four of them together create a rounded shape.

Breakfast buddies

These little guys know that breakfast is the most important meal of the day. Will you build your egg sunny-side up or scrambled? How many pancakes will you stack? The choice is yours!

Quarter-circle piece

WANT TO HEAR A GOOD YOLK?

Large eye piece

FRIED EGG

Round orange piece makes a great yolk

Two quarter-circle tiles make a smiley mouth

TOAST

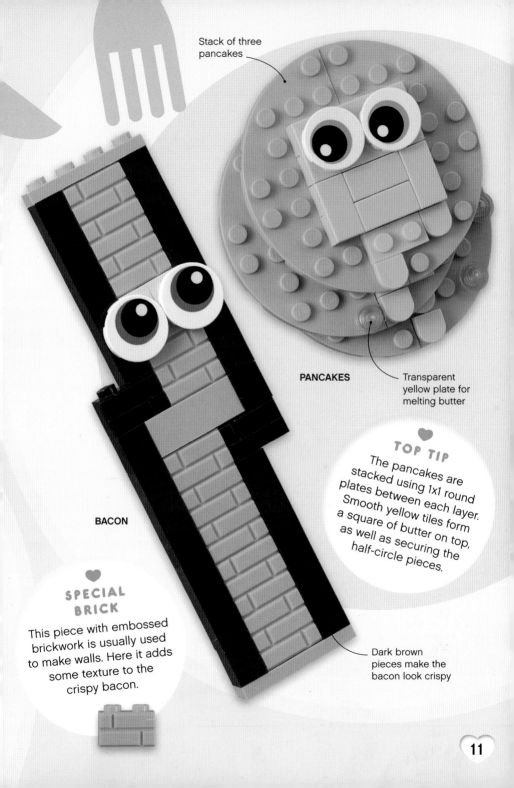

Stack of three pancakes

PANCAKES

Transparent yellow plate for melting butter

BACON

❤️
TOP TIP
The pancakes are stacked using 1x1 round plates between each layer. Smooth yellow tiles form a square of butter on top, as well as securing the half-circle pieces.

❤️
SPECIAL BRICK
This piece with embossed brickwork is usually used to make walls. Here it adds some texture to the crispy bacon.

Dark brown pieces make the bacon look crispy

Perfect pets

Have you always wanted a pet? How about a purple cat, a pink bunny, or a blue pug? Create your own perfect pet with LEGO® bricks in bright, kawaii colors.

Plate with bar allows ears to move

I'M THE MOST PURR-FECT PET AROUND...

Clips for handle to attach to

Antenna elements make whiskers

Tail swishes on a ball joint

Curved pieces for feet

CAT

Head can tilt inquisitively

SPECIAL BRICKS
The pug's tail is built onto a plate with a socket. The socket connects to a ball to allow the pug to happily wag his tail back and forth.

PUG

DON'T RABBIT ON ABOUT IT!

Ears are curved slope pieces with coral tiles inside

Heart-shaped tile makes a cute nose

BUNNY

13

Rain or shine

Whatever the weather, these sun and cloud symbols will be here to brighten up your day. Keep them on your windowsill and use them to show what the weather will be each day.

Flip this symbol up if it's raining outside, or lay it down flat if it's dry

Sky-blue bricks

Corner tile

Symbols attach to a 2x2 hinge top

FAIR-WEATHER FRIENDS

These cute weather symbols show if it's rainy, cloudy with some sunshine, or sunny. You could add other symbols, too, to show when it's windy, stormy, or snowing.

Cloud piece

Round orange plate makes a bright sun

Sleepy eyes

LOOKS LIKE IT'S GOING TO BE A BEAUTIFUL DAY!

Quarter-circle tiles

WEATHER SYMBOLS

Bag charms

These builds are simply charming! Make some cute bag charms to decorate your backpack. You could create candy, animal faces, or anything that makes you smile!

SPECIAL BRICK

This handy LEGO piece is a 2x4 brick with a key chain attached. Just add a few bricks to create a personalized bag charm.

3x3 plates without corners form the edge of the wrapper

Curved slope piece

BUNNY

CANDY IN A WRAPPER

Round tile for dog's nose

DOG

Boo!

There's no need to be spooked by these adorable ghosts—they just want to be friends! Build them onto transparent stick pieces so they look like they are floating.

TRICK OR TREAT!

Tooth pieces form closed eyes

This silly ghost is sticking its tongue out!

Cloud piece gives a floaty shape

TRY THIS

From zombies to vampires, werewolves to mummies, even creepy things can be kawaii! Why not create other sweet, spooky creatures to haunt your bedroom?

17

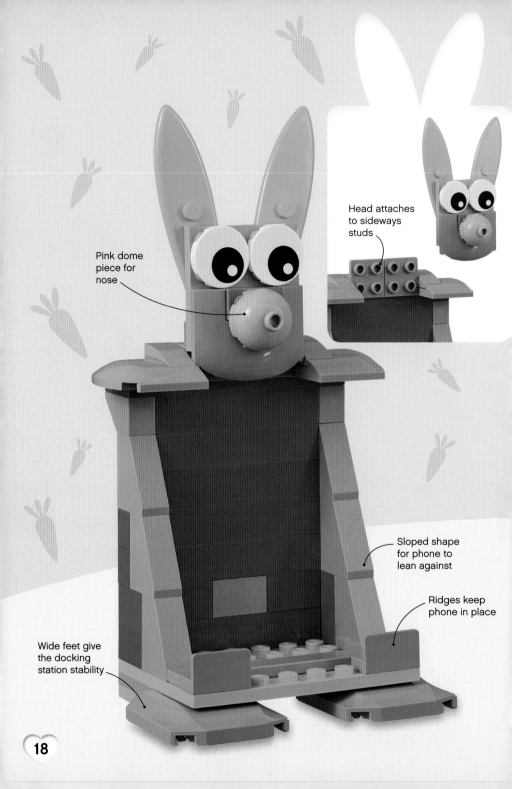

Pink dome piece for nose

Head attaches to sideways studs

Sloped shape for phone to lean against

Ridges keep phone in place

Wide feet give the docking station stability

Phone home

Give your phone a cool place to hang out while it charges with this bunny docking station. Why not swap the bunny ears for cat ears, or add a unicorn horn?

Long bunny ears

💜 **SPECIAL BRICK**

This LEGO® Friends surfboard has studs for a mini doll to stand on. Here, they attach to the model to form perfect bunny ears!

HAS ANYONE SEEN MY CHARGER?

19

Groovy garden

Create a LEGO garden with some colorful blooms in pretty tubs. These flowers don't need watering, and won't attract snails and slugs—unless you build some, of course!

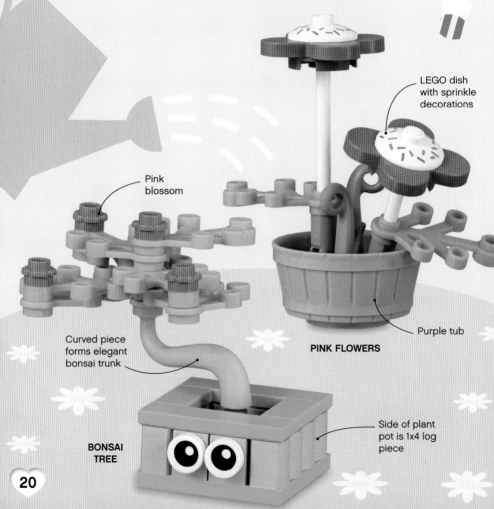

LEGO dish with sprinkle decorations

Pink blossom

Curved piece forms elegant bonsai trunk

PINK FLOWERS

Purple tub

Side of plant pot is 1x4 log piece

BONSAI TREE

Selfie time

Grab your friends and snap some fun selfies with these dress-up props. It's the perfect opportunity to try out a new look.

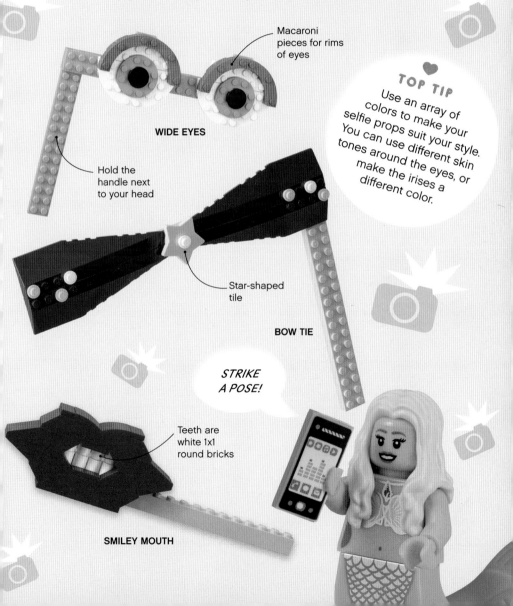

Macaroni pieces for rims of eyes

WIDE EYES

Hold the handle next to your head

TOP TIP

Use an array of colors to make your selfie props suit your style. You can use different skin tones around the eyes, or make the irises a different color.

Star-shaped tile

BOW TIE

STRIKE A POSE!

Teeth are white 1x1 round bricks

SMILEY MOUTH

Feathered friends

Squawk! Create a flock of birds to help chirp up your mornings. From parrots to sparrows, ducks to pigeons, there are many types of feathery friends you can build.

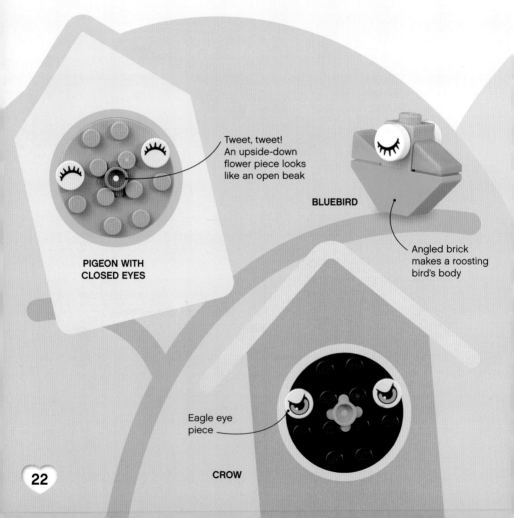

Tweet, tweet! An upside-down flower piece looks like an open beak

BLUEBIRD

PIGEON WITH CLOSED EYES

Angled brick makes a roosting bird's body

Eagle eye piece

CROW

Eyes and beak attach to bricks with side studs

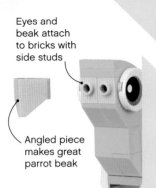

Angled piece makes great parrot beak

Large eye piece

PARROT

Tooth plate for beak

Sloped brick gives this bird a crest

SPARROW

WOODPECKER

Round plate

PIGEON WITH OPEN EYES

♥
TOP TIP
Your builds don't need to be three-dimensional. A round plate can be transformed into a happy, singing bird face! Just add eyes and a flower piece for the beak.

Snack break

There's nothing like a mid-morning snack to give you a little boost. Take a break with this sweet glass of chocolate milk and dancing cookie.

TOP TIP

Give your cookie legs so it can stand up and strike a funky pose. Build one leg onto the front of the model and the other one onto the back to add stability.

White and red round bricks make a striped straw

Brown plate adds a glimpse of chocolate milk

1x1 round plates for chocolate chips

Hands are plates with clips

Curved slopes give glass its shape

Sweet treats

These treats are not edible, but they are adorable!
Sprinkles or cherries, chocolate or icing, use your
LEGO bricks to whip up some fancy cakes to display.
What a treat for the eyes!

♥
TRY THIS

Make enough treats
to fill a whole bakery!
Why not build some pretty
macarons in pastel colors,
or some tarts decorated
with pieces of fruit?

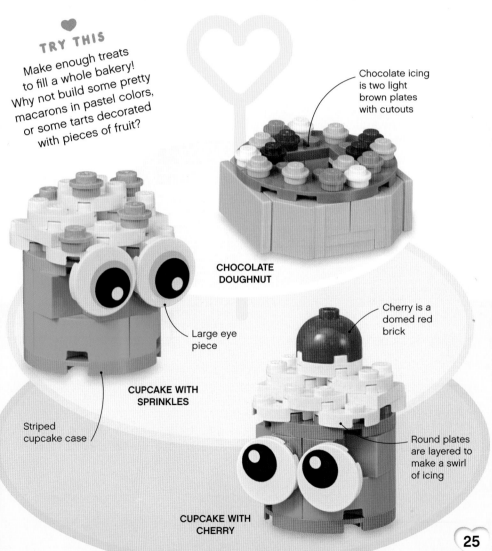

Chocolate icing
is two light
brown plates
with cutouts

**CHOCOLATE
DOUGHNUT**

Cherry is a
domed red
brick

Large eye
piece

**CUPCAKE WITH
SPRINKLES**

Striped
cupcake case

Round plates
are layered to
make a swirl
of icing

**CUPCAKE WITH
CHERRY**

Cute creatures

Build a collection of adorable animals to display in your bedroom. Go wild with flashy colors to really make your models pop!

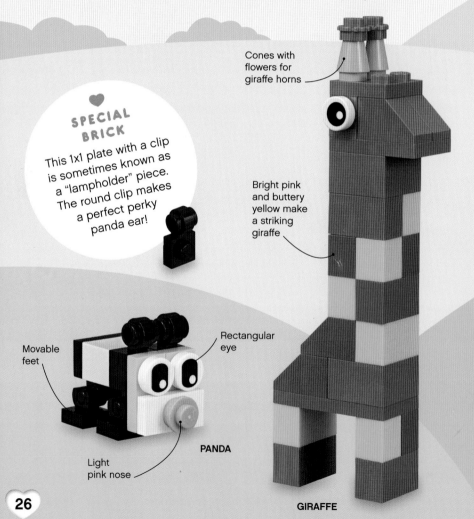

Cones with flowers for giraffe horns

Bright pink and buttery yellow make a striking giraffe

Movable feet

Rectangular eye

Light pink nose

PANDA

GIRAFFE

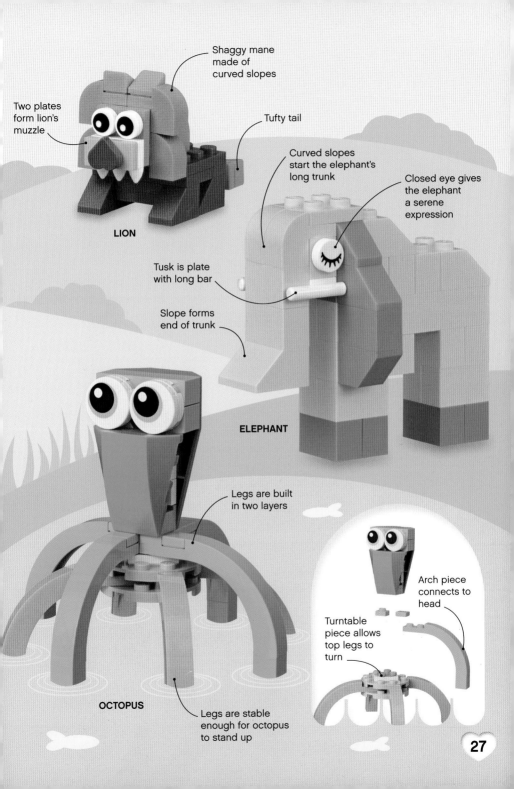

Shaggy mane made of curved slopes

Two plates form lion's muzzle

Tufty tail

Curved slopes start the elephant's long trunk

Closed eye gives the elephant a serene expression

LION

Tusk is plate with long bar

Slope forms end of trunk

ELEPHANT

Legs are built in two layers

Arch piece connects to head

Turntable piece allows top legs to turn

OCTOPUS

Legs are stable enough for octopus to stand up

Bricks are stacked in a staircase shape

White slopes add shape to the clouds

1x1 tiles form a pixelated curve

Sky-blue base plate

Smiley mouth is a macaroni tile

Cloud with sleepy eyes

Over the rainbow

Get your head in the clouds and build some magical rainbows. Whether they are two-dimensional, curved, or straight, the sky's the limit!

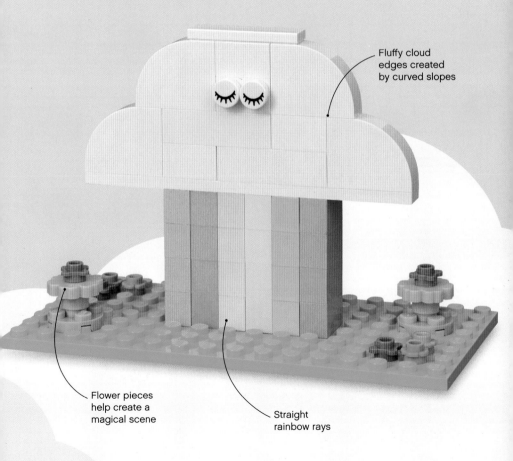

Fluffy cloud edges created by curved slopes

Flower pieces help create a magical scene

Straight rainbow rays

Box it up

Keep your treasures safe inside this zany, cute box. Decorated with colorful cogs, this savvy storage box will keep an eye out for anyone trying to steal your stuff.

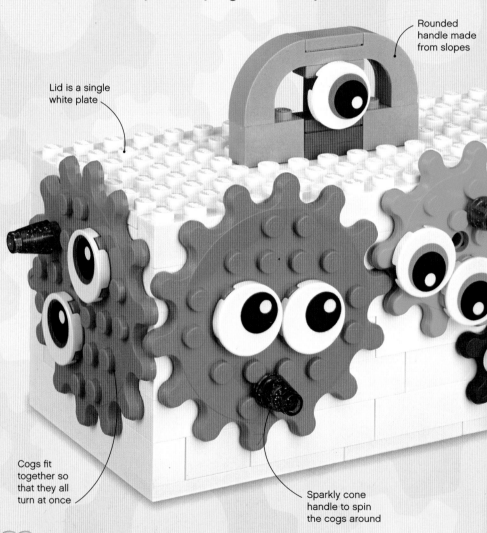

Rounded handle made from slopes

Lid is a single white plate

Cogs fit together so that they all turn at once

Sparkly cone handle to spin the cogs around

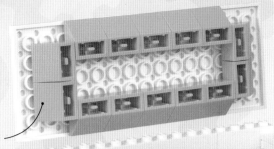

Lid sits flat
in this gap

Slopes keep
the lid in place

OPEN BOX

STORAGE SPACE

The box is hollow so you can
keep things inside. You could
use it to store other small builds
from this book!

LEGO Technic
brick and pin

Pin fits into
hole in the
center

♥
**SPECIAL
BRICK**

This colorful cog comes
in a LEGO® MOVIE 2™ set
and attaches with LEGO®
Technic pins. You could
use other LEGO cogs
in the same way.

Add a variety of
eye pieces to
give the cogs
personality

Happy birthday to you!

This bunch of balloons, brightly wrapped present, and tiered birthday cake are ready to celebrate. Anyone want to play musical chairs?

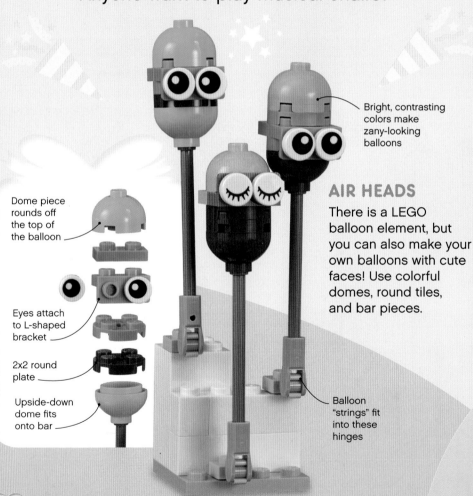

Bright, contrasting colors make zany-looking balloons

AIR HEADS

There is a LEGO balloon element, but you can also make your own balloons with cute faces! Use colorful domes, round tiles, and bar pieces.

Dome piece rounds off the top of the balloon

Eyes attach to L-shaped bracket

2x2 round plate

Upside-down dome fits onto bar

Balloon "strings" fit into these hinges

Two curved slopes make a bow

Smiley mouth made of tiles

PRESENT

♥
TOP TIP
Try making the present hollow so that there's room for a surprise inside! You could fill it with fun LEGO pieces, such as a croissant or a jewel element.

Flame piece tops the candle. Make a wish!

Jumper plate

THIS IS THE BEST BIRTHDAY EVER!

Yellow cake with pale purple icing

BIRTHDAY CAKE

33

Prehistoric pals

This Triceratops and Diplodocus roam the jungle together looking for snacks. These dinosaurs are vegetarians, so they'll need lots of leafy LEGO pieces to munch on.

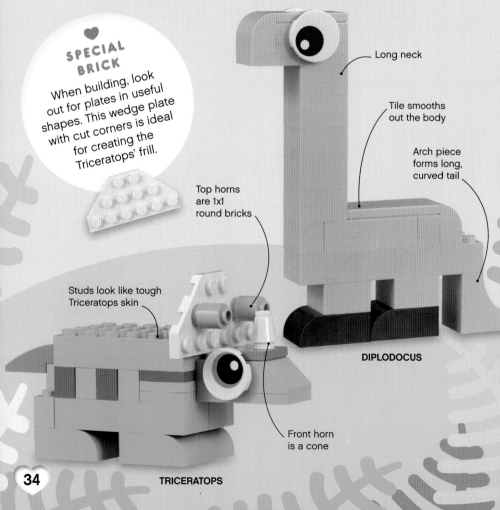

♥ SPECIAL BRICK

When building, look out for plates in useful shapes. This wedge plate with cut corners is ideal for creating the Triceratops' frill.

Long neck

Tile smooths out the body

Arch piece forms long, curved tail

Top horns are 1x1 round bricks

Studs look like tough Triceratops skin

DIPLODOCUS

Front horn is a cone

TRICERATOPS

Wise owls

These colorful owls have spent the day snoozing in their trees. Now that night is falling, they're wide awake and ready to fly.

Large eyes for spying tasty mice in the dark

TOP TIP

A variety of different types of slopes can be used to create wings, beaks, and ears. Mix it up depending on what bricks you have on hand.

1x1 curved slopes for ears

Colorful feathers

Brick with curved top attaches sideways for wing

Lunch time

Build a LEGO lunch box full of cute lunchtime snacks. This sandwich fits perfectly next to a shiny apple. And what lunch would be complete without a little carton of milk on the side?

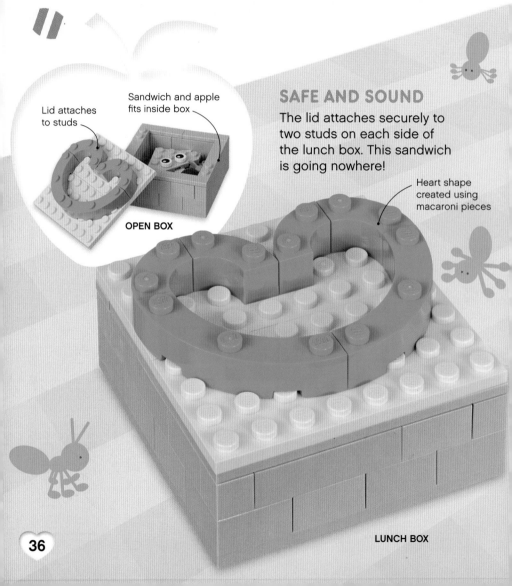

Lid attaches to studs

Sandwich and apple fits inside box

OPEN BOX

SAFE AND SOUND

The lid attaches securely to two studs on each side of the lunch box. This sandwich is going nowhere!

Heart shape created using macaroni pieces

LUNCH BOX

Tiles give a
smooth look

SUPER-CUTE SNACKS

Create recognizable milk
carton and sandwich shapes,
then add eye pieces for
kawaii appeal!

Leaf pieces are
layered with yellow
plate to make
sandwich fillings

MILK CARTON

Large eye piece
attached to
headlight brick

Apple is two
domes and
a leaf piece

Layered pieces
peek out from
the sides

Tan plates for
whole wheat
bread

SANDWICH

Stackable sushi

Dainty pieces of sushi are perfect kawaii creations. Give them faces, then stack them up ready to be dunked into some spicy wasabi and soy sauce.

SPECIAL BRICK

This piece is a flipper for a minifigure. Two of them placed side by side look like a shrimp tail!

Red piece for bottle top

SOY SAUCE

Orange round tiles and leaf piece for filling

Jumper plate allows these sushi pieces to stack

Striped shrimp

Black pieces look like shiny seaweed

MAKI

Green slopes make a swirl of wasabi

SHRIMP NIGIRI

Studs give the effect of bumpy grains of rice

Gray base plate for wasabi tray

WASABI

Say it with a symbol

Everyone knows a sprinkling of symbols adds sparkle to a message. Invent your own cute, two-dimensional symbols like this heart and star.

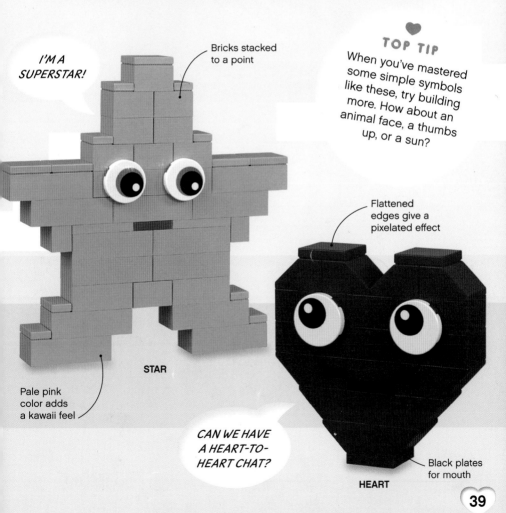

I'M A SUPERSTAR!

Bricks stacked to a point

TOP TIP
When you've mastered some simple symbols like these, try building more. How about an animal face, a thumbs up, or a sun?

Flattened edges give a pixelated effect

Pale pink color adds a kawaii feel

STAR

CAN WE HAVE A HEART-TO-HEART CHAT?

Black plates for mouth

HEART

Pretty plants

Plant an enchanted forest full of magical trees. Use brightly colored leaf pieces and add blossoms and birds to complete the scene.

Leaf pieces attach with clip

Four shafts for leaves to attach to

Round brick with hole forms the base

LEGO Technic pins connect the pieces

Angle connector

Bird can nestle on the leaf piece

Flower pieces fit into hinges

Studs so flowers or birds can be added

Wide base adds stability

PINK PALM TREE

PURPLE CHERRY BLOSSOM

THIS IS THE PERFECT UNICORN PARADISE!

Fruity faces

Make a fruit salad with prickly pineapples, juicy pears, and more! Don't forget to add eyes and a smile to give them their own personalities.

Curved pear stem

SPECIAL BRICK

This tuft of grass can be used to create lush green landscapes. It also makes perfect spiky pineapple leaves!

Eyes are set into model

Alternating yellow and orange pieces create sense of texture

PEAR

Lopsided smile

Stacked 1x1 round tiles for toothy smile

PINEAPPLE

Ribbit!

These frogs like to chill out on their favorite lily pads and wait for juicy flies to come along. Any fly that ventures too close is caught with a flick of a long froggy tongue. Yum!

SPECIAL BRICK

This piece is a minifigure roller skate. Add a transparent round tile to turn it into a fly. The wheels can be insect legs!

Calmly closed eye

Bright blue belly adds a kawaii touch

Slope creates squat frog body

THESE BIG BLUEBOTTLES ARE MY FAVORITE!

1x1 transparent round tile makes see-through fly wings

Happy
hedgehogs

Build a trio of hedgehogs in bright colors.
The studs on LEGO® bricks are perfect for
creating the appearance of spiky bodies.

Tan cone
forms long
snout

Flower piece
for nose

Layers of plates
form round body

Candyland

With just a few simple bricks in bright colors, you can build enough confectionery characters to fill a whole candy shop!

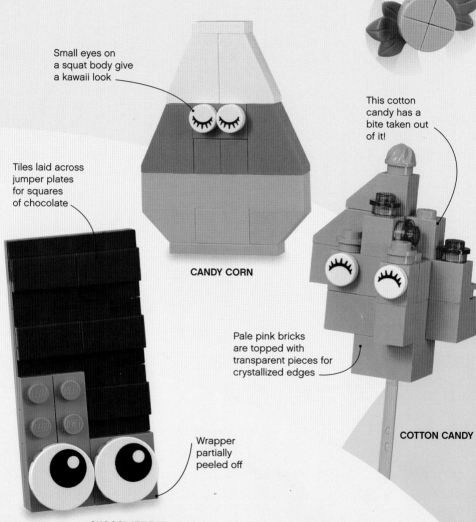

Small eyes on a squat body give a kawaii look

This cotton candy has a bite taken out of it!

Tiles laid across jumper plates for squares of chocolate

CANDY CORN

Pale pink bricks are topped with transparent pieces for crystallized edges

Wrapper partially peeled off

COTTON CANDY

CHOCOLATE BAR

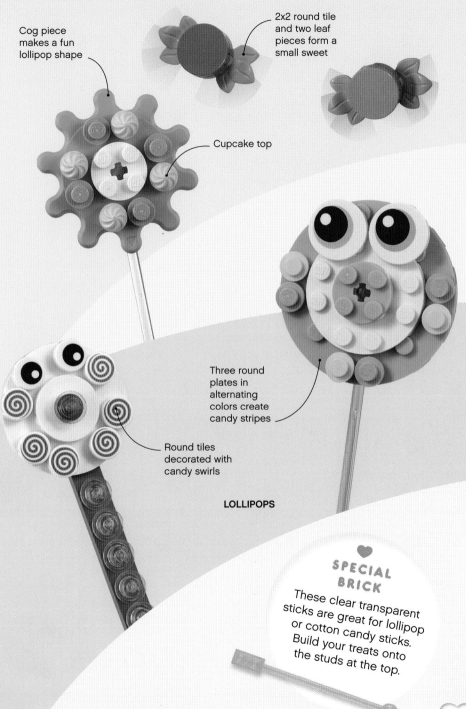

Cog piece makes a fun lollipop shape

2x2 round tile and two leaf pieces form a small sweet

Cupcake top

Three round plates in alternating colors create candy stripes

Round tiles decorated with candy swirls

LOLLIPOPS

♥
SPECIAL BRICK

These clear transparent sticks are great for lollipop or cotton candy sticks. Build your treats onto the studs at the top.

Fantasy creatures

Build the animal of your dreams! A colorful unicorn horn can be added to any animal build to transform it into a unique magical creature.

Green unicorn horn set into 1x1 round plate

Pink 1x1 slopes make cute unicorn ears

UNICORN

Overhanging edges make the mane and tail look thick and wavy

BACK VIEW

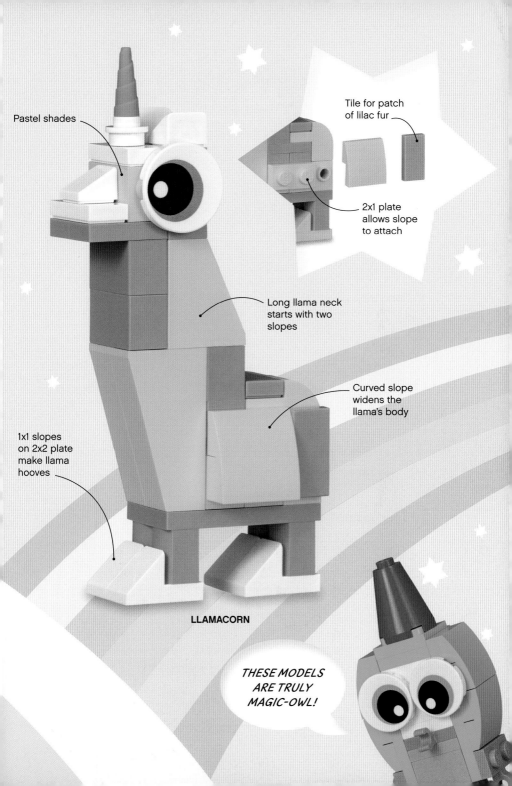

Pastel shades

Tile for patch of lilac fur

2x1 plate allows slope to attach

Long llama neck starts with two slopes

Curved slope widens the llama's body

1x1 slopes on 2x2 plate make llama hooves

LLAMACORN

THESE MODELS ARE TRULY MAGIC-OWL!

Closed eyes are perfect for a lazy sloth

Clawed hands

Dark brown and tan face

Plates with hinges stack to form a petite sloth nose

Eyes attach to headlight bricks

Brown slopes make long, muscular arms for hanging onto branches

Take it slow

There's nothing this sloth likes better than to unwind in its favorite tree. Its claws, made from gray hook pieces, allow it to climb to the highest branches.

Fabulous foxes

These fantastic foxes are ready to get up to all kinds of fun. Build them in realistic orange and white, or go wild with bright, kawaii colors.

Tip of nose is a 1x1 tile

White brick and slope make a proud fox chest

Round bricks make neat fox legs

Create a variety of expressions using different eye pieces

White-tipped tail

TOP TIP
Choosing just three or four colors per fox will give your builds more impact. Consider keeping the ears, nose, legs, and feet the same color.

ANY ROOM FOR ANOTHER FOX IN YOUR CLUB?

Brick-built pencils

Hollow cube with room for pencils

SPECIAL BRICK
This piece has a clip at one end so that it can attach to a bar. Here, three of them together make fingers for the pencil holder's hands.

TAKE NOTE OF THESE AMAZING BUILDS!

Teeth are white tiles built onto bricks with side studs

Two front teeth are built onto jumper plates so they stick out

Fingers attach to plate with bar

Legs are wide enough for pencil holder to stand without wobbling

PENCIL HOLDER

Stunning stationery

Never lose track of your stationery again with this friendly pencil holder. Build it a pencil and notepad to keep it company on your desk.

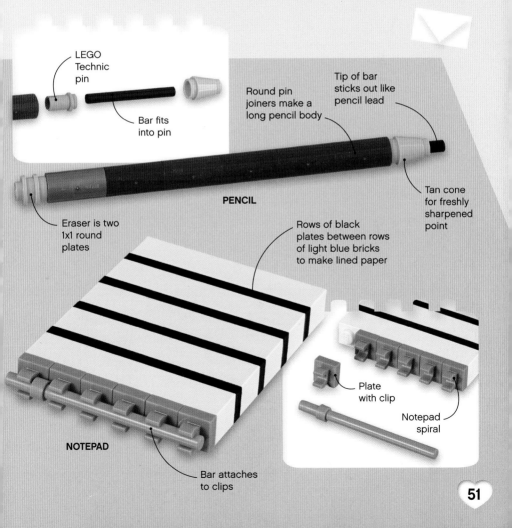

LEGO Technic pin

Bar fits into pin

Round pin joiners make a long pencil body

Tip of bar sticks out like pencil lead

Eraser is two 1x1 round plates

PENCIL

Tan cone for freshly sharpened point

Rows of black plates between rows of light blue bricks to make lined paper

Plate with clip

Notepad spiral

NOTEPAD

Bar attaches to clips

Healthy greens

Grow a whole garden of LEGO vegetables!
Use a mix of colors to create a bumper crop,
from fluffy broccoli to slender carrots.

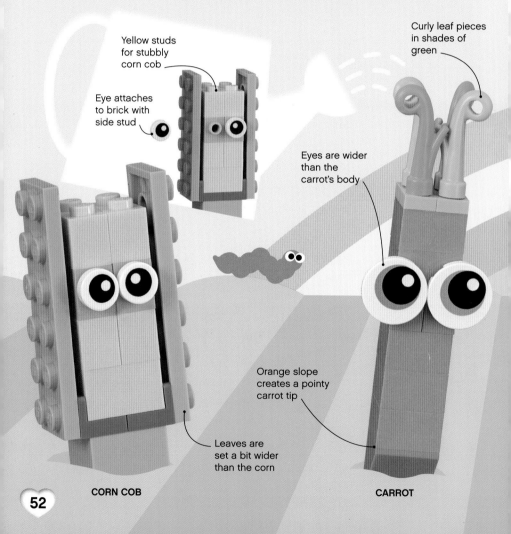

Yellow studs
for stubbly
corn cob

Eye attaches
to brick with
side stud

Curly leaf pieces
in shades of
green

Eyes are wider
than the
carrot's body

Orange slope
creates a pointy
carrot tip

Leaves are
set a bit wider
than the corn

CORN COB

CARROT

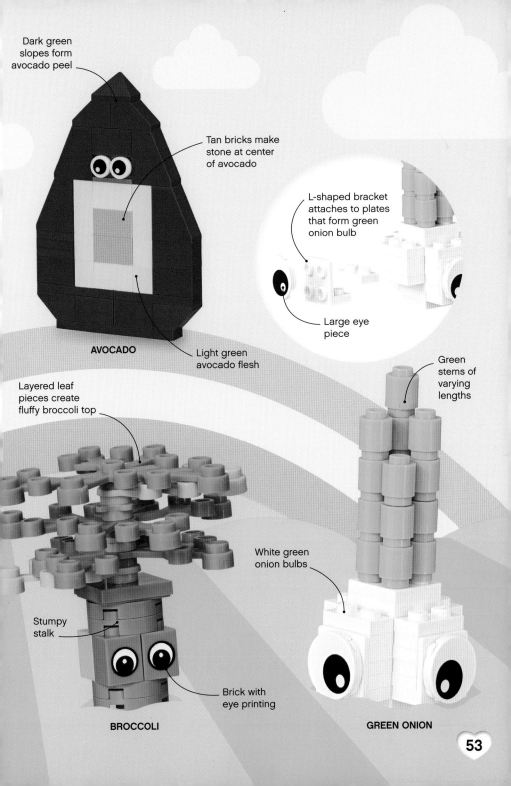

Dark green slopes form avocado peel

Tan bricks make stone at center of avocado

AVOCADO

Light green avocado flesh

L-shaped bracket attaches to plates that form green onion bulb

Large eye piece

Layered leaf pieces create fluffy broccoli top

Green stems of varying lengths

White green onion bulbs

Stumpy stalk

Brick with eye printing

BROCCOLI

GREEN ONION

Tiny rooms

Create some cozy miniature rooms. Just a few cleverly placed LEGO pieces can create household items like a shower, a lamp, or a quilt. Join the rooms together to make your dream home!

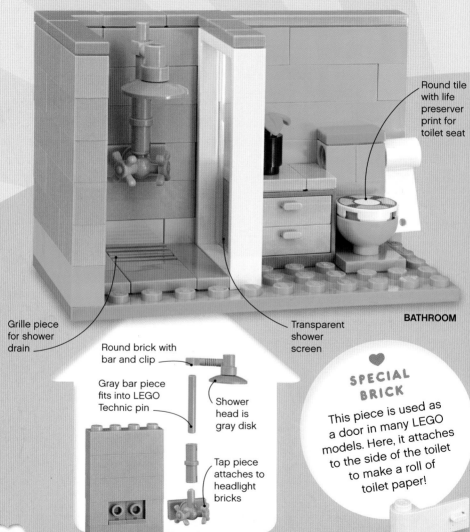

Round tile with life preserver print for toilet seat

BATHROOM

Grille piece for shower drain

Transparent shower screen

Round brick with bar and clip

Gray bar piece fits into LEGO Technic pin

Shower head is gray disk

Tap piece attaches to headlight bricks

SPECIAL BRICK

This piece is used as a door in many LEGO models. Here, it attaches to the side of the toilet to make a roll of toilet paper!

MINIFIGURE BEDROOM

Build a bedroom for your favorite minifigure. Decide on the color scheme and what items your minifigure would have in their room.

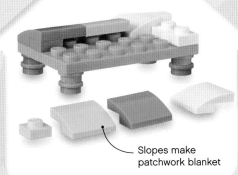

Use printed tiles as posters

Slopes make patchwork blanket

Sparkly cone makes fun lava lamp

Drawer is jumper plate

BEDROOM

THIS ROOM IS PERFECT FOR ME!

55

Invent a monster

There's no monster quite like this monster. It's truly one of a kind! Create your own unique monster using your LEGO bricks.

❤
TOP TIP

When building make-believe creatures, let your imagination run wild. Add extra arms or another head! Why not add scales or a tail, too?

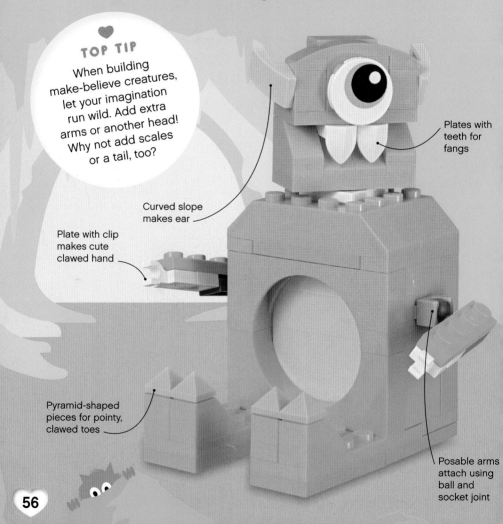

Plates with teeth for fangs

Curved slope makes ear

Plate with clip makes cute clawed hand

Pyramid-shaped pieces for pointy, clawed toes

Posable arms attach using ball and socket joint

Adorable
aliens

These space creatures are ready to welcome you with open tentacles to their home planet. What other space creatures can you build?

Alien tentacles are transparent plant pieces

Curly plant pieces for antennae

GREETINGS FROM EARTH! I COME IN PEACE.

Turntable piece allows head to turn

Flipperlike feet are leaf pieces

SPECIAL BRICK

This useful turntable piece is especially good for building characters with posable heads. It lets the head to turn from side to side.

Fast food

Take a trip to the diner with these fast-food friends. Build your meal in small, medium, or large, then choose a drink. Do you want fries with that? Will your burger contain pickles? You decide!

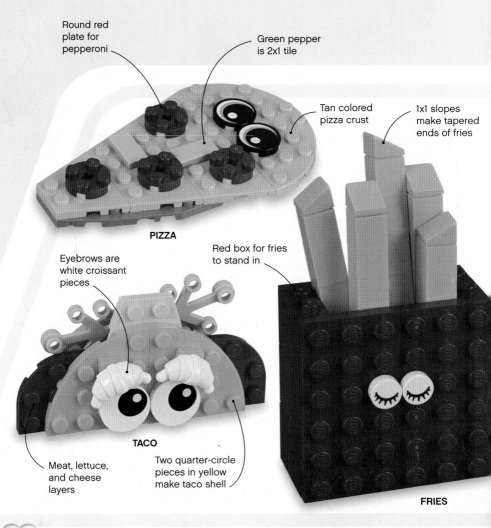

Round red plate for pepperoni

Green pepper is 2x1 tile

Tan colored pizza crust

1x1 slopes make tapered ends of fries

PIZZA

Eyebrows are white croissant pieces

Red box for fries to stand in

Meat, lettuce, and cheese layers

TACO

Two quarter-circle pieces in yellow make taco shell

FRIES

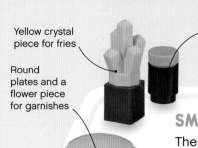

Yellow crystal piece for fries

Round plates and a flower piece for garnishes

Can of pop is just one round brick with one round tile

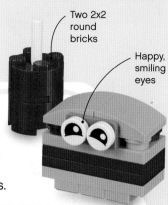

Two 2x2 round bricks

Happy, smiling eyes

SMALL BITES

There's more than one way to make a burger! Try some micro builds using just a few pieces.

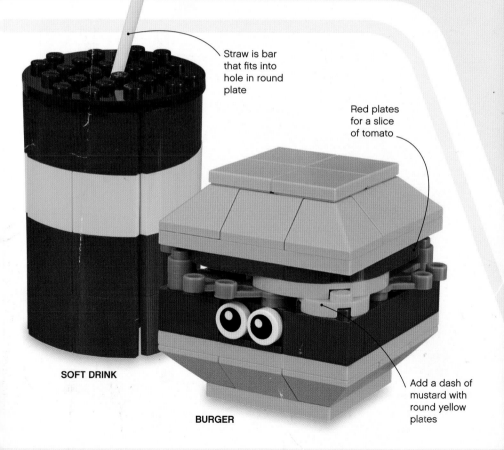

Straw is bar that fits into hole in round plate

Red plates for a slice of tomato

Add a dash of mustard with round yellow plates

SOFT DRINK

BURGER

Room for next face to stack on top

Stack 'em up

Build cat faces in different colors, leaving some studs free at the top so they can be stacked. Challenge a friend to see how high you can stack your builds.

Slope piece forms the start of the cat's muzzle

2x2 brick fits into space between the ears of the cat below

Whiskers can be pointed up or down

Jumper plate for nose to attach to

Fiery friend

This loyal dragon will guard your bedroom and breathe fire at any intruders! With his jointed tail and posable wings, he looks like he could take to the sky at any moment.

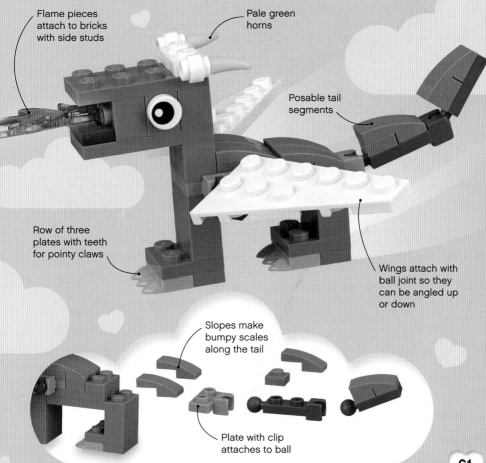

Flame pieces attach to bricks with side studs

Pale green horns

Posable tail segments

Row of three plates with teeth for pointy claws

Wings attach with ball joint so they can be angled up or down

Slopes make bumpy scales along the tail

Plate with clip attaches to ball

Happy hot dog

You've heard of a weiner dog, but how about a half-sausage, half-dog mash-up? This little guy loves walks in the park, but don't let him sizzle in the sun!

Cone forms nozzle of mustard bottle

Striped bottle top

MUSTARD

BBQ SAUCE

LOVE YOUR OUTFIT!

Curved slope for floppy dog ear

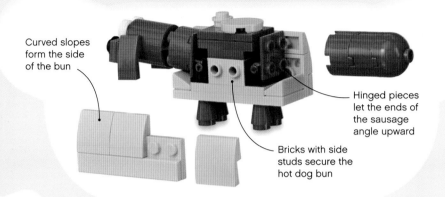

Curved slopes form the side of the bun

Hinged pieces let the ends of the sausage angle upward

Bricks with side studs secure the hot dog bun

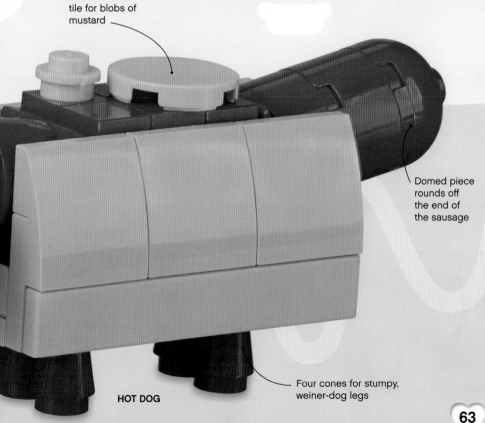

1x1 round plate and 2x2 round tile for blobs of mustard

Domed piece rounds off the end of the sausage

Four cones for stumpy, weiner-dog legs

HOT DOG

Need
for speed

Travel in style with these mini vehicles! Whether by road or by sky, these adorable vehicles can nip to the scene in no time.

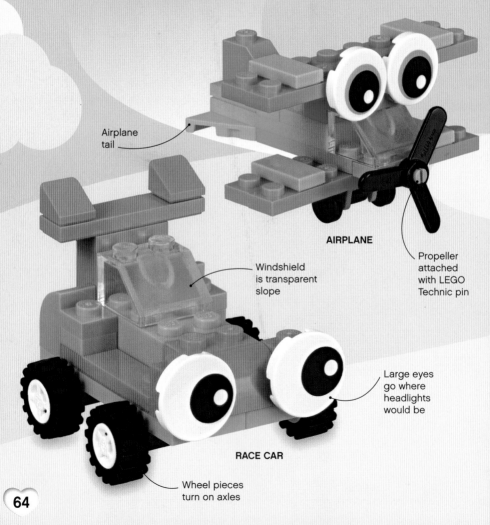

Airplane tail

AIRPLANE

Windshield is transparent slope

Propeller attached with LEGO Technic pin

Large eyes go where headlights would be

RACE CAR

Wheel pieces turn on axles

Rotor piece spins on the pin

Plate with pin

HELICOPTER

Landing skids are two 3x1 plates

Ladder piece attached on hinge at rear

♥
TOP TIP

There are plenty of LEGO wheel pieces to choose from when you build your vehicles. If you don't have any wheels, a black 2x2 round plate will work.

Tools can clip onto the side of the fire truck

Transparent yellow plates serve as headlights and also as the fire truck's cheeks!

FIRE TRUCK

Play it cool

On a hot day, what could be better than a refreshing ice pop or an ice cream cone with tasty toppings? These colorful, icy treats with cute cartoon faces are ready for fun in the sun!

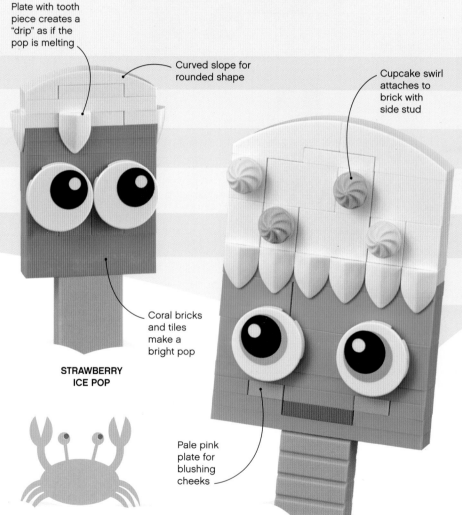

Plate with tooth piece creates a "drip" as if the pop is melting

Curved slope for rounded shape

Cupcake swirl attaches to brick with side stud

Coral bricks and tiles make a bright pop

STRAWBERRY ICE POP

Pale pink plate for blushing cheeks

BLUE ICE POP

TRY THIS

Why not build enough treats to fill a whole ice cream van? Experiment with shapes and colors to make bomb pops, ice cream sandwiches, snow cones, and more.

Slopes in bright colors for scoops of ice cream

Don't forget the toppings!

This pop has a bite taken out of it!

ICE CREAM CONE

Watermelon seed is 1x1 round tile

Bite shape is created by staggered plates topped by tiles

Plate with clip makes a silly tongue

Tan ridged piece for stick

WATERMELON ICE POP

Sweet music

This dinky drum and colorful guitar are ready for a jam session. Why not build some more musical instruments to join in the fun?

Cupcake swirl acts as end of drumstick

Clip holds the drumstick

Arm is plate with bar at either end

SPECIAL BRICK

This antenna is useful for all kinds of technology-themed models. Here, it makes a great "whammy bar" for a guitar.

Grille pieces placed end to end for guitar strings

Plates with angled edges gives guitar its distinctive shape

Posable arms so drum can beat itself

Drum is built onto round plate

DRUM

GUITAR

Garden
pals

Even the simplest of builds can be adorable! Make a family of slugs and snails. Give each of them a unique personality by using different pieces for their shells and tentacles.

Cupcake top gives the impression of a swirly snail shell

Antenna pieces can be angled forward to make a grumpy snail!

Studs look like snail's tentacles

Cones topped with 1x1 round plates are another way to make tentacles

TOP TIP
Once you've built your slugs and snails, why not add more cute and colorful garden creatures, like striped bees or spotted ladybugs?

2x2 round brick with flower piece makes a jazzy shell

Slopes make good slug bodies

DK Penguin Random House

EDITOR Rosie Peet
US EDITOR Megan Douglass
SENIOR DESIGNER Lauren Adams
DESIGNERS Elena Jarmoskaite and Ray Bryant
SENIOR PRE-PRODUCTION PRODUCER Marc Staples
SENIOR PRODUCER Louise Daly
MANAGING EDITOR Paula Regan
MANAGING ART EDITOR Jo Connor
PUBLISHER Julie Ferris
ART DIRECTOR Lisa Lanzarini
MODEL PHOTOGRAPHY Gary Ombler

MODELS CREATED BY
Emily Corl and Rod Gillies

Dorling Kindersley would like to thank Randi Sørensen, Heidi K. Jensen, Paul Hansford, Martin Leighton Lindhardt, Nina Koopmann, Charlotte Neidhardt, and Torben Vad Nissen at the LEGO Group; Lisa Robb for design work and concept development; Julia March at DK for proofreading; and Elena Jarmoskaite, Lauren Adams, and Rosie Peet at DK for additional models.

First American Edition, 2020
Published in the United States by DK Publishing
1450 Broadway, Suite 801, New York, NY 10018

Copyright ©2020 Dorling Kindersley Limited
DK, a Division of Penguin Random House LLC
20 21 22 23 24 10 9 8 7 6 5 4 3 2 1
001–315803–June/2020

A catalog record for this book is available from the Library of Congress.

ISBN 978-0-7440-2150-9

Printed and bound in China

A WORLD OF IDEAS:
SEE ALL THERE IS TO KNOW

www.dk.com
www.LEGO.com

MEET THE BUILDERS

EMILY CORL

Emily loves bright colors so these models are a true reflection of herself! Her favorites are the fire truck and airplane. Her tip for cute builds is to keep them simple and give them lots of expression.

ROD GILLIES

Rod had great fun on this book because it prompted him to experiment outside his usual style. He really enjoyed building the hot dog because the idea made him laugh!